An act for widening and repairing the road from Combebridge, in the county of Somerset, to Bradford, in the county of Wilts; and from thence, through Hilperton, and so far over Ashton Common

An act for widening and repairing the road from Combebridge, in the county of Somerset, to Bradford, in the county of Wilts; and from thence, through Hilperton, and so far over Ashton Common, as to join the road which leads from Steeple-Ashton to Trowbridge; and also the road leading from Bradford aforesaid to Cockhill-gate, in the said county of Wilts.

Multiple Contributors, See Notes
ESTCID: T224379
Reproduction from Bodleian Library (Oxford)
Enacted: Public General Acts, 25 Geo.II.c.52. Drop-head title.
[London?] : Printed in the year, 1752.
61,[1]p. ; 8°

ECCO
ECCO

Eighteenth Century
Collections Online
Print Editions

Gale ECCO Print Editions

Relive history with *Eighteenth Century Collections Online*, now available in print for the independent historian and collector. This series includes the most significant English-language and foreign-language works printed in Great Britain during the eighteenth century, and is organized in seven different subject areas including literature and language; medicine, science, and technology; and religion and philosophy. The collection also includes thousands of important works from the Americas.

The eighteenth century has been called "The Age of Enlightenment." It was a period of rapid advance in print culture and publishing, in world exploration, and in the rapid growth of science and technology – all of which had a profound impact on the political and cultural landscape. At the end of the century the American Revolution, French Revolution and Industrial Revolution, perhaps three of the most significant events in modern history, set in motion developments that eventually dominated world political, economic, and social life.

In a groundbreaking effort, Gale initiated a revolution of its own: digitization of epic proportions to preserve these invaluable works in the largest online archive of its kind. Contributions from major world libraries constitute over 175,000 original printed works. Scanned images of the actual pages, rather than transcriptions, recreate the works *as they first appeared.*

Now for the first time, these high-quality digital scans of original works are available via print-on-demand, making them readily accessible to libraries, students, independent scholars, and readers of all ages.

For our initial release we have created seven robust collections to form one the world's most comprehensive catalogs of 18th century works.

Initial Gale ECCO Print Editions collections include:

History and Geography
Rich in titles on English life and social history, this collection spans the world as it was known to eighteenth-century historians and explorers. Titles include a wealth of travel accounts and diaries, histories of nations from throughout the world, and maps and charts of a world that was still being discovered. Students of the War of American Independence will find fascinating accounts from the British side of conflict.

Social Science

Delve into what it was like to live during the eighteenth century by reading the first-hand accounts of everyday people, including city dwellers and farmers, businessmen and bankers, artisans and merchants, artists and their patrons, politicians and their constituents. Original texts make the American, French, and Industrial revolutions vividly contemporary.

Medicine, Science and Technology

Medical theory and practice of the 1700s developed rapidly, as is evidenced by the extensive collection, which includes descriptions of diseases, their conditions, and treatments. Books on science and technology, agriculture, military technology, natural philosophy, even cookbooks, are all contained here.

Literature and Language

Western literary study flows out of eighteenth-century works by Alexander Pope, Daniel Defoe, Henry Fielding, Frances Burney, Denis Diderot, Johann Gottfried Herder, Johann Wolfgang von Goethe, and others. Experience the birth of the modern novel, or compare the development of language using dictionaries and grammar discourses.

Religion and Philosophy

The Age of Enlightenment profoundly enriched religious and philosophical understanding and continues to influence present-day thinking. Works collected here include masterpieces by David Hume, Immanuel Kant, and Jean-Jacques Rousseau, as well as religious sermons and moral debates on the issues of the day, such as the slave trade. The Age of Reason saw conflict between Protestantism and Catholicism transformed into one between faith and logic -- a debate that continues in the twenty-first century.

Law and Reference

This collection reveals the history of English common law and Empire law in a vastly changing world of British expansion. Dominating the legal field is the *Commentaries of the Law of England* by Sir William Blackstone, which first appeared in 1765. Reference works such as almanacs and catalogues continue to educate us by revealing the day-to-day workings of society.

Fine Arts

The eighteenth-century fascination with Greek and Roman antiquity followed the systematic excavation of the ruins at Pompeii and Herculaneum in southern Italy; and after 1750 a neoclassical style dominated all artistic fields. The titles here trace developments in mostly English-language works on painting, sculpture, architecture, music, theater, and other disciplines. Instructional works on musical instruments, catalogs of art objects, comic operas, and more are also included.

bibliolife
old books. new life.

The BiblioLife Network

This project was made possible in part by the BiblioLife Network (BLN), a project aimed at addressing some of the huge challenges facing book preservationists around the world. The BLN includes libraries, library networks, archives, subject matter experts, online communities and library service providers. We believe every book ever published should be available as a high-quality print reproduction; printed on-demand anywhere in the world. This insures the ongoing accessibility of the content and helps generate sustainable revenue for the libraries and organizations that work to preserve these important materials.

The following book is in the "public domain" and represents an authentic reproduction of the text as printed by the original publisher. While we have attempted to accurately maintain the integrity of the original work, there are sometimes problems with the original work or the micro-film from which the books were digitized. This can result in minor errors in reproduction. Possible imperfections include missing and blurred pages, poor pictures, markings and other reproduction issues beyond our control. Because this work is culturally important, we have made it available as part of our commitment to protecting, preserving, and promoting the world's literature.

GUIDE TO FOLD-OUTS MAPS and OVERSIZED IMAGES

The book you are reading was digitized from microfilm captured over the past thirty to forty years. Years after the creation of the original microfilm, the book was converted to digital files and made available in an online database.

In an online database, page images do not need to conform to the size restrictions found in a printed book. When converting these images back into a printed bound book, the page sizes are standardized in ways that maintain the detail of the original. For large images, such as fold-out maps, the original page image is split into two or more pages

Guidelines used to determine how to split the page image follows:

• Some images are split vertically; large images require vertical and horizontal splits.
• For horizontal splits, the content is split left to right.
• For vertical splits, the content is split from top to bottom.
• For both vertical and horizontal splits, the image is processed from top left to bottom right.

AN
ACT
FOR

Widening and Repairing the Road from Combebridge, *in the County of* Somerset, *to* Bradford, *in the County of* Wilts; *and from thence, through* Hilperton, *and so far over* Ashton Common, *as to* join *the Road which leads from* Steeple-Ashton *to* Trowbridge; *and also the Road leading from* Bradford *aforesaid to* Cockhill-gate, *in the said County of* Wilts.

Printed in the YEAR M.DCC.LII.

An ACT *for Widening and Repairing the Road from* Combe-bridge, *in the County of* Somerset, *to* Bradford, *in the County of* Wilts; *and from thence through* Hilperton; *and so far over* Ashton Common, *as to join the Road which leads from* Steeple Ashton *to* Trowbridge; *and also the Road leading from* Bradford *aforesaid to* Cockhill-gate, *in the said County of* Wilts.

WHEREAS the Road leading from that End of Combe-bridge which joins the Bath Road, in the County of Somerset, to and through Winsley and Bradford; and from thence over Ferneat's Common and Mitchell Mead to Staverton Bridge, through

A 2

Hilperton, down *Guy's-Lane*, and so far over *Ashton-Common*, as to join the Road which leads from *Steeple Ashton* to *Troughbridge*, and also the Road leading from *Bradford* Bridge to a Place called *Cockvill-gate*, in the County of *Wilts*, are in many Places, from the Nature of the Soil, and by reason of the many heavy Carriages passing thereon, become deep and ruinous, and in several other Parts are too narrow for Carriages to pass by each other, and other Parts of the aforesaid Roads are frequently overflowed by the River *Avon*; and, for want of sufficient Drains and Bridges, are many times, and especially in the Winter-season, rendered impassable for Horses and Carriages, to the great Danger of Travellers, and the Disappointment, Prejudice, and Loss, of the Woollen Manufacturers, and other Traders, as well by the Damage of their Goods, as also by the Delay in the Carriage and Conveyance of the same, and the said Roads cannot be effectually widened, amended, and kept in sufficient Repair, without the Aid and Authority of Parliament.

May it therefore please Your MAJESTY,

That it may be Enacted; And be it Enacted, by the KING's most Excellent Majesty, by and with the Advice and Consent of the Lords Spiritual and Temporal, and Commons, in this present Parliament assembled, and by the Authority of the same, That the Right Honourable *Edward Seymour*, commonly called Lord *Seymour*; the Right Honourable *Webb Seymour*, commonly called Lord

Trustees Names

Lord *Webb Seymour*, the Right Honourable
William Seymour, commonly called Lord *Wil-*
liam Seymour, the Right Honourable and Re-
verend *Francis Seymour*, commonly called Lord
Francis Seymour, the Right Honourable
Harry Powlett, commonly called Lord *Harry*
Powlett, the Honourable *Robert Herbert*,
Efquire, Sir *Robert Long*, Baronet, *Jeremiah*
Awdry, *Ambrose Awdry*, Liquires, *Peter Ba-*
thurst, *Thomas Beach*, *William Beach*, *John*
Bythefea, Burton, Liquires, *Richard*
Burcombe, *Thomas Cooper*, *John Cooper*, *Henry*
Coulthurst, Efquires, *Robert Cooper*, *George*
Cooper, *Samuel Cam*, *Nicholas Cam*, *William*
Clark, Doctor in Phyfick, *Peter Delme*,
George Dike, Efquires, *John Dyke*, of *Sarum*;
the Reverend *Ramfden Dawett*, *John*
Eyles, Efquire; *William Eyres*; *George F....*
Henry Eyles, Efquire, *Henry Effer*; *Jos*
Gerth, *James Gibbs*, Efquires, *Richard ....*
William Gardner, *Anthony Grey*, *P.....*
James Gibbs junior; *Jos.ell .. et S....*
John Halliday, *Robert Harwood*, *... Har-*
ding, Efquires, *Robert H.....*, *R..ert*
Hiffey, *George H.s.ton*, *.... est.. ...'y*
Augufline Hoit r, *W.... ..... Je.n*
Hetchings, the *Reverend L...r ....*, *Wil-*
liam Jones, Apothecary, *R.b.rt Jues*,
Thomas Jolisfer, *Rich. H...g*, *R.... H..g*,
junior, *Thomas L..r*, *Robert L..*, *H.... ..s*
Long, Liquires, the Reverend *John Lewis*;
William Ler, *David Ler*, *..... .... La Roux*,
Wadham Lock; *Paul Methuen*, *....ard Hru-*
tins, *James Metague*, *..... Mey*,
Efquires, *Edward Nurfes*, *Robert N.ve*,
Efquires,

Efquires, *Edward Popham*, *Edward Poore* of
Sarum, *Edward Poore* of *Bradford*, *John
Powell*, Efquires, the Reverend *William
Pryer*, *William Pen e*, Apothecary, *John
Pitman*, *Stephen Phelps*, *Seeker Roberen*,
Efquire, the Reverend *John Rogers*, the
Reverend *Jo. Rogers* junior, *Thomas Ro-
gers*, *William Read*, *Samuel Reynolds*, *John
Smith* of *Slow*, *Robert Smith*, *Lewis Sene*,
Jacob Selfe, *Prince Sutton*, *Zachariah Sha-
nel*, Efquires, the Reverend *Sparrow*, *William Sallman*, *Samuel Storing*, *Henry
Slade*, *John Stone*, *John Soath*, *Zachariah
Shrapnel* junior, *Thomas Spencer*, *Thomas
Slate*, *John Ivory Talbot*, *——Talbot*, *John
Turner*, *Richard Trick*, Efquires, *Humphry
Tugwell*, *Haine*, *Henry Walters*,
George Wills, *William Wills*, Efquires, *——
Stone*, *Richard Wbatly*, *James Wilms*,
Thomas Tisbury, *Joseph Tisbury*, Shirb.,
and they are hereby nominated and appointed,
Truftees for furveying, ordering, amending,
and keeping in Repair, the faid Roads, and
that they, and the Survivors of them, or any
Seven or more of them, or fuch Perfon or
Perfons as they, or any Seven or more of
them, fhall authorize and appoint, fhall and
may build and erect, or caufe to be built and
erected, a Gate or Gates, Turnpike or Turnpikes, in, upon, or acrofs, or at the Sides of
any Part or Parts of the faid Roads, and alfo a
Tollhoufe or Tollhoufes in or upon the
fame, other than and except as is herein after-
mentioned, and otherwife provided, and
fhall demand and take the Tolls and Du-

following, before any Horfe, Mare, Gelding, Mule, Afs, Cattle, Coach, Landau, Chariot, Berlin, Chaife, Hearfe, Calafh, Chair, Waggon, Wain, Cart, or other Curriage whatfoever, fhall be permitted to pafs through the fame, that is to fay, For every Coach, Berlin, Landau, Chariot, Calafh, Chaife, Hearfe, or Litter, drawn by Four or more Horfes, Mares, Geldings, or Mules, One Shilling, and drawn by Two Horfes, Mares, Geldings, or Mules, Six pence. For every Calafh, Chaife, or Chair, drawn by One Horfe, Mare, Gelding, or Mule, Three-pence. For every Waggon, Wain, Cart, or other Curriage, drawn by Two or more Horfes, Mares, Geldings, Oxen, or other Beafts of Draught, the Sum of One Shilling, and drawn by Four Horfes, Mares, Geldings, Oxen, or other Beafts of Draught, Two-pence, and drawn by One Horfe, Mare, Gelding, Ox, or other Beaft of Draught, Six-pence a Toll or Duty, and the Money, so to be raised and collected, shall be, and is hereby, vested in the several Trustees, and the same, and every Part thereof, shall be paid, applied, and disposed of, and assigned, to and for the several Uses, Intents, and Purposes, and in such Manner, as is herein after-mentioned and directed.

And it is hereby further Enacted, That it shall and may be lawful to and for the said Trustees, or any Five or more of them, or any such Person or Persons as they, or any Five or more of them, under their Hands and Seals, shall, from time to time, nominate and appoint to demand and take the Tolls and Duties hereby granted, and made payable, to levy the same upon any Person or Persons who shall, after Demand thereof made, neglect or refuse to pay such Tolls and Duties, as aforesaid, by Distress of any Horse or Horses, or other Cattle or Goods, upon which such Tolls or Duties are by this Act imposed, or by Distress of any other of the Goods and Chattels of such Person or Persons who ought to pay the same, and to detain and keep the same, until such Tolls or Duties, with the reasonable Charges of such Detaining and Keeping, shall be paid: And it shall and may be lawful to and for such Person or Persons so distraining, after the Space of Five Days after such Distress made and taken (such Toll or Duty, with the reasonable Charges of such Detaining and Keeping, not being then paid),

paid), to fell the Goods fo diftrained and detained, returning the Overplus (if any there be), upon Demand, to the Owner thereof, after fuch Tolls, Duties, and reafonable Charges of diftraining and keeping the fame, fhall be firft deducted and paid.

Provided always, and be it further Enacted, by the Authority aforefaid, That no Perfon fhall be capable of acting as a Truftee, in any Cafe, in the Execution of this Act, unlefs he fhall be, in his own Right, or in the Right of his Wife, in the actual Poffeffion or Enjoyment of Lands, Tenements, or Hereditaments, of the yearly Value of Fifty Pounds, or fhall have perfonal Eftate alone, or real and perfonal Eftate together, to the Value of One thoufand Pounds; or fhall be Heir-apparent to fome Perfon or Perfons having an Eftate of the yearly Value of Two hundred Pounds And if any Perfon or Perfons, fo made incapable to act, for the Caufes aforefaid, fhall neverthelefs prefume to act, contrary to the true Intent and Meaning of this Act, every Perfon or Perfons, for fuch Offence, fhall forfeit and pay the Sum of Fifty Pounds to any Perfon or Perfons that fhall inform, and fue for the fame, to be recovered in any of his Majefty's Courts of Record, by Action of Debt, or on the Cafe, Bill, Plaint, or Information; wherein no Effoign, Protection, Wager of Law, or more than One Imparlance, fhall be allowed

And

No Tolls on E-lection-Days.

And it is hereby further Enacted, Declared, and Provided, That, during the Continuance of this Act, all Coaches, Berlins, Landaus, Chariots, Chaises, Calashes, Chairs, or Litters, and Passengers on Horseback, going to, or returning from, the Election of a Knight or Knights of the Shire to serve in Parliament for the several Counties of *Wilts* and *Somerset*, shall, on the Day appointed for such Elections, and also on the Day before, and the Day after, such respective Elections, pass and repass Toll-free through the said Turnpikes or Toll-gates, or any of them; any thing herein contained to the contrary notwithstanding.

How the M ney bor owed on the Tolls is to be applied

And be it further Enacted, by the Authority aforesaid, That out of the first Money arising by the Tolls and Duties, which shall be collected at the several Turnpikes so to be erected on the Roads aforesaid, or out of such Money which shall be borrowed on the Credit thereof, the Trustees for repairing the said Roads directed to be amended, or any Five or more of them, shall, in the First place, pay and discharge all the Expences and Charges of procuring and passing this Act of Parliament, and of putting up and erecting such Turnpikes and Toll houses as they shall think proper, on the said Roads, and that, from and after paying the said Expences and Charges, then, and from thenceforth, the Money arising by the Tolls and Duties which shall be collected at any Turnpike or Turnpikes,

pikes, which fhall be then or hereafter erected
or fet up on the faid Roads, fhall be laid
out and applied for and towards the Repairing of the faid Roads, and other neceffary
Charges attending fuch Repairs, and for fuch
other Purpofes as are herein after-mentioned.

Provided always, and it is hereby
Enacted and Declared, That if the
faid Truftees, and the Survivors, or any
Five or more of them, fhall think requi-
fite to erect and fet up, or caufe to be
erected and fet up, a Turnpike and Toll-
gate at or near *Hilperton* Marfh Gate, or
between the fame Gate and *Staverton* Bridge,
lying and being on the faid Road: And in fuch
cafe, if that Part of the Road from *Trowbridge* to *Staverton*, which lies through *Hilperton* Marfh, cannot be kept in fufficient
Repair, by the ordinary Courfe of Law, in
the Judgment and to the Satisfaction of the
Truftees who may be appointed by an Act of
this prefent Seffion of Parliament, for repairing the Road from the Top of *Tinhead Hill*,
in the County of *Wilts*, to *Mitford*, in the
County of *Somerfet*, to be fignified in Writing, under the Hands of any Five or more
of them, and delivered to the Clerk of the
Truftees to be appointed in purfuance and
for the Purpofes of this prefent Act; then,
and in fuch Cafe, the laft-mentioned Truftees, or their Succeffors, or any Five or more
of them, fhall pay, or caufe to be paid, out
of the Tolls or Duties arifing by virtue of
this prefent Act, any Sum, not exceeding, in
the Whole, the yearly Sum of Five Pounds,

to

to the Surveyors of the Highways of the several Parishes or Places wherein *Hilperton* Marsh is situate and being, in proportion to the Extent of the said Road, within such Parishes respectively, to be by them respectively applied and disposed of, for and towards the repairing the said Road in and over the same Marsh.

And it is hereby further Enacted and Declared, That it shall and may be lawful to and for the Trustees appointed for the Purposes of this present Act, and their Successors, or any Five or more of them (in case they shall think it requisite or necessary), out of the Money to be raised and levied, by virtue and in pursuance of this Act, to lay out and apply, or order to be laid out and applied, any Sum or Sums of Money, not exceeding the Sum of Five Pounds, in any One Year, for repairing and amending the Road leading from *Staverton* Bridge to *Holt*, in the Parish of *Bradford*

And be it further Enacted, by the Authority aforesaid, That if any Person or Persons whatsoever, owning, renting, or occupying, any Lands, Grounds, or Tenements, near to any Turnpike which shall be erected in pursuance of this Act, shall, knowingly or wittingly, permit or suffer any Person or Persons to pass through any Gate, Passage, or Way, with any Coach, Chaise, Chariot, Landau, Berlin, Calash, Waggon, Wain, Cart, or other Carriage, Horse, Ass, Mule,

or

or any Sort of Cattle, whereby the Payment of the Tolls or Duties by this Act laid shall be avoided, every such Person so offending, and also the Person thereby avoiding the Payment of the said Toll, and being thereof convicted, upon Oath or Affirmation, before the said Trustees, or any Five or more of them, (who are hereby impowered to administer such Oath), or before any One or more Justice or Justices of the Peace for the said County of *Wilts* (which Oath the said Justice or Justices is and are hereby impowered to administer), shall, for every such Offence respectively, forfeit and pay to the Trustees authorized to put this Act in Execution, or to their Treasurer or Treasurers for the Time being, the Sum of Twenty Shillings, which Sum, in case the same be not forthwith paid, shall be levied by Distress and Sale of the Offender's Goods, by Warrant under the Hand and Seal, or Hands and Seals, of the said Trustees, or any Five or more of them, or of such Justice or Justices, rendering the Overplus to the Owner (if any be), on Demand, after deducting the reasonable Charges of making such Distress and Sale, to be settled by the said Trustees, or any Five or more of them, or by the said Justice or Justices.

And be it further Enacted, by the Authority aforesaid, That if any Person or Persons shall, at any time during the Continuance of this Act, unload, or cause to be unloaden, any Sort of Goods or Merchandizes, or take off, or cause to be taken off, any Horse or Ho ses,

To prevent the unloading of Goods or Horses, and the Payment of Toll.

Horses, from any Coach, Chariot, Berlin,
Landau, Chaise, Calash, Chair, Hearse, or
Litter, or any Horse or Horses, Ox or Oxen, or
other Cattle, from any Waggon, Wain, Cart,
or other Carriage, at or before the same shall
come to any of the Gates or Turnpikes
erected by virtue of this Act, with an Intent
to avoid paying any of the Tolls or Duties,
hereby imposed, or shall conceal or secrete
any Goods, or other Things chargeable with
any of the Tolls aforesaid, or shall put or
leave in any House, or Place any Coach,
Chariot, Berlin, Landau, Chaise, Calash,
Chair, Waggon, Wain, Cart, or any other
Carriage, Horse, Gelding, Mare, or any
other Cattle, chargeable with, or liable to
pay, the said Tolls or Duties, with such Intent
as aforesaid, each and every Person, so offending in any of the Gates aforesaid, shall forfeit
and pay, to the Trustees appointed, or to be
appointed, to put this Act in Execution, or
to their Treasurer for the Time being, the
Sum of Twenty Shillings, which shall be recovered and levied, and applied, as any
other Penalties or Forfeitures are to be recovered and levied, and applied, by virtue of
this Act.

And be it further Enacted, by the Authority aforesaid, That it shall and may be
lawful to and for the said Trustees, or any
Five or more of them, to erect, or cause to be
erected, One or more Gate or Gates, Turnpike or Turnpikes, Toll-house or Toll-houses,
on the Side or Sides of the said Roads, and

cross any Lane or Way leading out of the same, and there to take and receive such Tolls as are by this Act granted, and made payable, so as the same do not extend to a double Charge, in case of passing through any other of the Turnpikes which shall be erected by virtue of this Act.

Provided always, and it is hereby Enacted and Declared, That no Turnpike or Toll-gate shall be erected, or set up, by, or by Order of, the said Trustees, or any of them, in or upon any Part of the Road directed and appointed by this Act to be repaired, which lies between *Bidbrooke-Gate*, in the said Road, and *Cock-hill-Gate* aforesaid, or in or upon any Part of the said Road which lies between that Lrd of *Gamlebridge* which joins the *Bath* Road, and the House that is now inhabited by Master *Harry Fisher*, in the same Road, or in or upon any Part of the said Road which lies between the West End of the House at *Hilperton*, called or known by the Name or Sign of the *Lamb and Fiddle*, and the North-East Corner of *Guy's-Lane* aforesaid.

And be it further Enacted, by the Authority aforesaid, That the said Trustees, or any Seven or more of them, present at their First or any succeeding Meeting, by any Writing under their Hands and Seals, shall and may choose and appoint One or more fit Person or Persons to be Clerk or Clerks, Treasurer or Treasurers, Receiver or Receivers, Collector or Collectors, of the Tolls and Duties afore-

aforesaid, and also One or more fit Person or
Persons to be Surveyor or Surveyors, to view
the Condition of the said Roads, and to see
that the same is repaired; and also that the
Money, by this Act raised, be duly applied,
and, from time to time, to remove such Clerks,
Treasurers, Collectors, Receivers, and Surveyors, or any of them, as they shall see Occasion, and appoint new ones, in case of
Death, or such Removal. And such Person or
Persons as is or are hereby made liable to pay
the said Tolls or Duties, shall pay the same,
after the Rates aforesaid, to such Treasurer
or Treasurers, Receiver or Receivers, Collector or Collectors, as shall, from time to
time, be appointed for that Purpose. And
the Person or Persons so appointed to collect
and receive the said Tolls or Duties, and
also such Surveyor and Surveyors so appointed as aforesaid, shall, upon Oath, or,
being of the People called *Quakers*, upon
their solemn Affirmation, if thereunto required by the said Trustees, or any Five or
more of them, or before One or more Justice
or Justices of the Peace, residing near the said
Roads (which Oath or Affirmation the said
Trustees, or any Five or more of them, or
such Justice or Justices, is and are hereby impowered and required to administer), and
also shall, on the First *Wednesday* in every
Month, or oftener, if required, during the
Continuance of this Act, give a true, exact,
and perfect Account, in Writing, under their
respective Hands, of all Moneys which he
and they, and every or any of them, shall to

such

such time have received, paid, and disbursed, by virtue of this Act, or by reason of their respective Offices, for which Oath no Fee or Reward shall be taken, and the same may be taken in Writing, without any Stamp thereupon. And in case any Money, so received, shall remain in their or any of their Hands, the same shall be paid to the said Trustees, or any Five or more of them, or to such Person or Persons as they, or any Five or more of them, shall, by any Writing or Writings, under their Hands, authorize and empower to receive the same, and shall be disbursed and laid out in amending the said Roads, according to the true Intent and Meaning of this Act, and not otherwise. And the said Trustees, or any Five or more of them, shall and may, out of the Money arising by the said Tolls or Duties, make such Allowance to the Clerk or Clerks, Treasurer or Treasurers, Receiver or Receivers, Collector or Collectors, and the Surveyor and Surveyors, and other Officers, by the said Trustees, or any Five or more of them, so appointed as aforesaid, for and in Consideration of his and their Care and Pains respectively taken in the Execution of his and their said respective Office or Offices, and to such other Person or Persons as have been, or shall be, assisting in and about procuring the said Road to be amended and repaired, by advancing or laying out any Money, or otherwise, relating thereunto, as to the said Trustees, or any Five or more of them, shall seem good. And in case the said Receiver or Receivers, Col-

And setting the Salaries of their Officers.

Penalties on Officers not giving in their Accounts,

lector

C

and making Pay-
ments. lector or Collectors, of the aforesaid Tolls or Duties, so to be paid as aforesaid, or any of them, shall not give and make such Account and Payment, as the said Trustees, or any Five or more of them, shall order and direct, that then any Two or more Justices of the Peace of the said County of *Wilts*, at any Special Sessions, or Monthly Meeting of them to be holden for the said County, shall make Inquiry of or concerning such Default, as well by Confession of the Parties themselves, as by the Testimony of One or more credible Witness or Witnesses, upon Oath (which Oath the said Justices are hereby impowered and required to administer, without Fee or Reward) And if any Person or Persons shall be thereof convicted by such Justices, the said Justices shall, upon such Conviction, commit the Party or Parties to the common Gaol of the County of *Wilts*, there to remain, without Bail or Mainprize, until he, she, or they, shall have made a true and perfect Account, and Payment, as aforesaid, or shall have compounded and agreed with such Trustees, and paid such Composition to the said Treasurer or Treasurers, for the Time being, which Composition the said Trustees respectively, or any Five or more of them, at any Meeting assembled, are hereby authorized and impowered to make

Powers to Sur-
veyors, &c. **And be it further Enacted,** by the Authority aforesaid, That it shall and may be lawful to and for the said Surveyor or Surveyors, and such Persons as he or they

shall

shall appoint, to dig, gather, take, and carry
away, any Gravel, Furze, Heath, Sand,
Stones, or other Materials, out of any River
or Brook, or out of or from the Waste
or Common, of or in any Parish, Town,
Tything, Village, or Hamlet, in the said
several Counties proper and convenient for
Repairing and Amending of the Roads aforesaid, and, for want of sufficient Gravel, Furze,
Heath, Sand, Stones, or other Materials,
there, to dig, gather, take, and carry away
the same, in and out of any River, Brook,
Waste or Common, of any neighbouring Parish, Town, Village, or Hamlet, in any other
County or Counties, without paying any
thing for the same, such Surveyor or Surveyors levelling, or causing to be levelled,
all such Holes and Pits where any such Materials, as aforesaid, shall be digged, gathered or
taken, and from whence the same shall be
carried away. And where there is not sufficient of such Materials in any such Rivers,
Brooks, Commons, or Waste-grounds, as
aforesaid, it shall and may be lawful to and
for such Surveyor or Surveyors, by Order of
the said Trustees, or any Five or more of
them, to dig and gather such Materials in,
and carry the same out of, the several Grounds
of any Person or Persons (not being the
Ground whereon any Houses stand, or a
Garden, Orchard, Yard, or Park, planted
Walk or Walks, or Avenue to any House,
or any Piece or Parcel of Ground set apart
or used as a Plantation or Nursery for Trees),
where such Materials are or may be found;

B 2   and

and, from time to time, to carry away the same, or so much thereof as the said Surveyor or Surveyors shall judge necessary for repairing and amending the Roads aforesaid; paying such Rates for such Materials, and for the Damage done to the Owners and Occupiers respectively of the Grounds, where and from whence the same shall be digged, gathered, or carried away, or over which the same shall be carried, as the said Trustees appointed or to be appointed for repairing the said Roads, or any Five or more of them, shall adjudge reasonable. And in case of any Difference concerning the same, between such Owners or Occupiers, and the said Trustees, touching such Damages, as aforesaid, the Justices of the Peace, at their next General Quarter-Sessions, to be holden in and for the said County of *Wilts*, or the major Part of them present, shall and may adjudge, assess, and finally determine the same.

Make Satisfaction to the Owners.

And be it further Enacted, by the Authority aforesaid, That it shall and may be lawful to and for the Surveyor or Surveyors, and such Person or Persons as he or they shall appoint (by the Direction of the said Trustees, or any Five or more of them, under their Hands), from time to time, to remove and prevent all Annoyances on or in any Part of the Roads aforesaid, by Filth, Dung, Ashes, Rubbish, or otherwise, and to turn any Watercourses, Sinks, or Drains, running into, along, or out of the said Roads, to the Prejudice thereof, and to cleanse, open, scour,

Surveyors may remove Annoyances.

drain, deepen, or enlarge, any Ditch or
Watercourse adjoining to the said Roads, and
to cut down, lop, or top, any Trees or Bushes
('Timber-trees excepted) growing in the said
Roads, or in the Hedges or Banks adjacent
thereto, and to take and carry away the
same (the Owners or Occupiers of the Premises where such Annoyances, as aforesaid,
shall happen to be, neglecting to remove the
same), and to cut down such Trees (except
as before excepted) or Bushes, or to remove
such other Annoyances, for the Space of Ten
Days next after Notice in Writing given for
that Purpose, under the Hands of the said
Trustees, or any Five or more of them, the
Charges whereof shall be reimbursed to the
said Surveyor or Surveyors, by such Owners
or Occupiers neglecting to cut down such
Trees or Bushes, or to remove such other
Annoyances, as aforesaid · And if, after Removal of the said Annoyances, any Person
or Persons shall again offend in the like
kind, every Person so offending, and being
thereof convicted upon Oath before One or
more Justice or Justices of the Peace for the
said County of *Wilts*, shall, for every such Offence, forfeit and pay unto the said Trustees,
or their Treasurer for the Time being, the
Sum of Twenty Shillings, to be levied in
manner herein after mentioned.

And be it further Enacted, by the Authority aforesaid, That it shall and may be
lawful to and for the said Surveyor or Surveyors, and such Person or Persons as they

B 3   shall

shall appoint, by Order of the said Trustees, or any Five or more of them, to make, or cause to be made, Causeways, and to cut and make Drains through any Grounds lying contiguous to the said Roads, and to make and erect Arches or Bridges of Brick, Timber, or Stone, upon the said Roads, and also to widen any of the narrow Parts of the said Roads, by opening, clearing, and laying into the same, any Grounds of any Person or Persons, lying contiguous thereto (not being the Ground whereon any House or Houses stand, or Garden, Orchard, planted Walk, or Avenue to any House already planted, or Nursery for Trees), and also to cause Ditches or Trenches to be made in such manner, as such Surveyor or Surveyors, by Order of the said Trustees, or any Five or more of them, shall judge necessary for the better amending and keeping the Roads aforesaid in good Repair, making such reasonable Satisfaction to the Owners and Occupiers of such Ground respectively, as shall be so laid in or unto the said Roads, or through which any such Drain or Ditch shall be cut, or on which any such Arch or Arches, Bridge or Bridges, shall be made, for the Damages which such Owners or Occupiers respectively shall or may thereby sustain, as shall be adjudged by the said Trustees, or any Five or more of them And, in case any Difference shall happen between such Owners or Occupiers and the said Trustees, touching such Damages, that then it shall and may be lawful to and for the Justices of the Peace, at

their

their next General Quarter-Seffions to be holden
for the faid County of *Wilts*, or the major Part
of fuch Juftices then prefent, to hear, fettle,
adjudge, and finally determine the fame And
if any Owner or Owners, Occupier or Occupiers, of any Watercourfe or Watercourfes,
Ditch or Ditches, adjoining to the faid Roads,
fhall neglect or refufe to fcour and cleanfe fuch
Watercourfe or Watercourfes, or to make fuch
Ditch or Ditches fo deep, and in fuch manner, as
the Surveyor or Surveyors hereby appointed,
or to be appointed, fhall, from time to time,
judge proper and convenient, after Ten Days
Notice fhall be given, for that Purpofe, by
fuch Surveyor or Surveyors, or fuch Perfon
or Perfons as he or they fhall appoint, to
fuch Owner or Owners, Occupier or Occupiers, it fhall and may be lawful to and for
fuch Surveyor or Surveyors to fet any Man
or Men at Work to fcour and cleanfe the
fame, and by Warrant from any Three or
more of the faid Truftees, to levy the Charges
thereof upon the Goods or Eftates of the
Owner or Owners, Occupier or Occupiers, of
fuch Watercourfe or Watercourfes, Ditch or
Ditches, by Diftrefs and Sale of his, her, or
their Goods and Chattels, rendering the Overplus, if any be, after all Charges of fuch
Levying, Keeping, and Selling, thereout
deducted, to the faid Owner or Owners,
Occupier or Occupiers, when by him, her,
or them, demanded

And be it further Enacted, by the Authority aforefaid, That it fhall and may be

lawful

lawful for the faid Surveyor or Surveyors, by Order of the faid Truftees, or any Seven or more of them, to make, or caufe to be made, a Road or Way through, over, or along, any Grounds adjoining to any narrow or ruinous Part or Parts of the faid Roads hereby intended to be repaired (not being the Grounds whereon any Houfes or Buildings ftand, or a Garden, Orchard, Yard, Park, planted Walk or Walks, or Avenue to any Houfe, or any Piece or Parcel of inclofed Ground, planted, fet apart, and ufed as a Plantation or Nurfery for Trees), to be made ufe of by all Paffengers with Horfes, Coaches, Carriages, or otherwife, as a publick Highway, whilft the old, narrow, or ruinous Road, is repairing, and till fuch time as it fhall be convenient and fafe for Paffengers and Carriages to travel and go along the faid Road intended to be

Making Satif-faction repaired, and no longer, making fuch reafonable Satisfaction to the Owners or Occupiers of fuch Grounds refpectively, as fhall be fo laid in or unto the faid Road, or through which any Drain or Drains fhall be cut, or on which any Arch or Arches, Bridge or Bridges, fhall be made, or through, over, or along which fuch temporary Road or Roads fhall be made, for the Damage fuch Owners or Occupiers refpectively fhall or may fuftain thereby, as fhall be adjudged by the faid Truftees, or any Seven or more of them And in cafe any Differences fhall happen between fuch Owners or Occupiers, and the faid Truftees, touching fuch Damages, that then it fhall and may be lawful to and for the Juf-

tices

tices of the Peace, at their next General
Quarter-Sessions, or at their Second Quarter-
Sessions at the farthest, to be holden for the
said County of *Wilts*, or the major Part of
them present at such Quarter-Sessions, and
they are hereby required, to hear, settle, adjudge, and finally to determine the same.

And forasmuch as the Money to be collected by Receipts of the Tolls or Duties by
this Act made payable, as aforesaid, will not,
for some time, be sufficient for the effectual
Repairing of the said Roads, **Be it enacted**
Enacted, by the Authority aforesaid, That
the said Trustees, or any Seven or more of
them, shall, may, and are hereby impowered, from time to time, by any Writing
under their Hands and Seals, to assign over
the said Tolls and Duties arising by virtue of
this Act, or any Part thereof (the Costs and
Charges of assigning the same to be borne
and paid out of such Tolls and Duties), for
any Time or Term during the Continuance
of this Act, as a Security for the Payment of
such principal Sum or Sums of Money as shall
be borrowed by the said Trustees for that Purpose, unto the Person or Persons respectively,
who shall advance and lend the same, together
with lawful Interest, or less, as shall be agreed
upon, which said Money, so to be borrowed,
shall be applied and disposed of, as the said
Tolls or Duties by this Act are directed to be
applied and disposed of, and to no other Use
or Purpose whatsoever.

And be it further Enacted, by the Authority aforesaid, That Copies of all and every the Assignment or Assignments, so to be made by the said Trustees, as aforesaid, shall be entered at Length, in a Book or Books, to be kept for that Purpose, by the said Clerk or Clerks, Treasurer or Treasurers, which said Book or Books shall and may be seen and perused at all seasonable times, by any Person or Persons whomsoever, without Fee or Reward.

Provided always, and it is hereby Declared and Enacted, by the Authority aforesaid, That no Person or Persons, having Occasion to pass through any Turnpike or Turnpikes where the Tolls or Duties are or shall be taken, and who shall return the same Day through the same Turnpike or Turnpikes, before Twelve of the Clock in the Night of that Day, with the same Coach, Berlin, Chariot, Landau, Calash, Chaise, Chair, Hearse, Litter, Waggon, Wain, Cart, or other Carriage, Horse, Gelding, Mare, Mule, Ass, or any Sort of Cattle, for which such Tolls or Duties have been paid, shall be liable or compelled, the same Day, to pay the said Tolls and Duties more than once

And be it further Enacted, by the Authority aforesaid, That, in case the said Trustees appointed or to be appointed to put this Act in Execution, or any Twelve or more of them, shall, from time to time, think

think proper to turn or alter the Way or
Path, or any Part of the faid Road hereby
directed to be repaired, for the better Accom-
modation of Coaches, Carriages, and Paffengers, that then it shall and may be lawful
to and for the faid Truftees, or any Twelve or
more of them, and they are hereby authorized
and impowered, from time to time, to purchafe,
or agree for any Lands or Grounds, lying contiguous to the faid Road, of the Owners or
Proprietors thereof (if fuch Owners or Proprietors fhall be willing to fell and difpofe of
the fame), and to pay for the fame out of
the Tolls and Duties by this Act granted, or
out of the Money by them to be borrowed
on the Credit thereof, fuch Sum or Sums of
Money by them to be borrowed on the Credit thereof, fuch Sum or Sums of Money as
fhall be agreed upon between fuch Owners
or Proprietors, and the faid Truftees, or any
Twelve or more of them, to be paid for the
Purchafe of fuch Lands and Grounds, with
the Cofts and Charges attending fuch Purchafe
or Purchafes, and fuch Lands and Grounds,
when purchafed, as aforefaid, fhall, by Order
and Direction of the faid Truftees, or any
Twelve or more of them, be laid into, and
made Part of, the faid Roads directed to be
amended by this Act, in fuch manner as the
faid Truftees, or any Twelve or more of
them, fhall think convenient, and fhall, by
them, or fuch Perfon or Perfons as they, or
any Twelve or more of them, fhall order
and appoint, be fufficiently ditched or fenced
out for that Purpofe, and, after the faid Lands
and

and Grounds fhll be fo ditched and fenced
out, the fame fhall, not only during the Continuance of this Act, but fhall for ever thereafter, to all Intents and Purpofes, be efteemed

and taken as publick Highways, and fhall be
amended, and kept in Repair, by fuch Ways,
and in fuch Manner, as other Ways are
amended, and kept in Repair, by the Laws in

being, and after fuch Purchafe fhall be made,
as aforefaid, the Lands and Grounds comprifed
in, or conftituting the old or former Road, in
lieu whereof the Land or Ground for fuch
new Road or Way fhall be purchafed, obtained, and made, as aforefaid, fhall or may
be fold or difpofed of by the faid Truftees,
or any Twelve or more of them, to fuch Perfon or Perfons as fhall be willing to become
Purchafers thereof, for the beft Price that can
be reafonably had or gotten for the fame,
and the Money arifing by fuch Sale fhall be
applied and difpofed of for the Repairing and
Amending the faid Roads, and fuch Conveyance or Conveyances to be made of the
faid Lands and Grounds comprifed in the
faid old Road, being executed by the faid
Truftees, or any Twelve or more of them,
and inrol'ed with the Clerk of the Peace for
the faid County of *Wilts*, fhall be good and
effectual in the Law, to all Intents and Purpofes whatfoever.

And whereas it may happen, that fome
Perfons, or Bodies Politick, Corporate, or
Collegiate, Feoffees in Truft, or others, are
feifed or poffeffed of fome Lands, Grounds,
Tene-

Tenements, or Hereditaments, which, according to the Powers given by this present Act, may, by the said Trustees, be thought necessary or proper to be taken in and added to the said Roads, either for extending, widening, enlarging, turning, altering, or amending, the same, as aforesaid, and they may be willing to treat and agree to sell such Lands, Grounds, Tenements, and Hereditaments, for the Purposes aforesaid, but are incapable of granting, selling, or conveying the same, by reason of Infancy, or other Disability, Be it therefore Enacted, by the Authority aforesaid, That it shall and may be lawful to, and for all Bodies Politick, Corporate, or Collegiate, Corporations Aggregate or Sole, and all Feoffees in Trust, Executors, Administrators, Guardians, or other Trustees whatsoever, for or on behalf of any Infants, Femes Covert, or Cestuique Trusts, and for all and every Person and Persons whatsoever, who are or shall be seised, possessed of, or interested in, any such Lands, Grounds, Tenements, or Hereditaments, to treat, contract, and agree, with the said Trustees, or any Twelve or more of them, for Satisfaction to be made them respectively for such their Lands, Grounds, Tenements, and Hereditaments, or any Part thereof, or their Interest therein, for the Purpose aforesaid, and to sell and convey the same, Occasion shall be or require And that all Contracts, Agreements, Sales, and Conveyances, which shall be made, shall be valid to all Intents and Purposes, any Statute, Usage, or any other

Matter

Matter or Thing whatſoever, to the contrary thereof in any-wiſe notwithſtanding And that all Feoffees in Truſt, Executors, Adminiſtrators, Guardians, and Truſtees, Corporations Corporate or Collegiate, Aggregate or Sole, and all other Perſons, are and ſhall be hereby indemnified for what they ſhall do by virtue or in purſuance of this Act

And it is hereby further Enacted, That if any ſuch Owner, Proprietor, Occupier, Body Politick, Corporate, or Collegiate, or other Perſon or Perſons, intereſted in ſuch Lands, Grounds, Tenements, or Hereditaments, upon convenient Notice to be given, or left in Writing, at the Dwelling-houſe or Place of Abode of ſuch Perſon or Perſons, or of the Head-Officer or Officers of ſuch Bodies Politick, Corporate, or Collegiate, or at the Houſe of the Tenant in Poſſeſſion of the Lands, Grounds, Tenements, and Hereditaments, ſo to be taken into, and added to, the ſaid Roads, as aforeſaid, or into which ſuch Way, Path, or Road, ſhall be turned or altered, as aforeſaid, ſhall, by the Space of Thirty Days after ſuch Notice given or left, as aforeſaid, neglect or refuſe to treat, or ſhall not agree in the Premiſes, or, by reaſon of Abſence, ſhall be prevented from treating, then, and in every or any ſuch Caſe, the ſaid Truſtees, or any Twelve or more of them, ſhall cauſe it to be inquired into, and aſcertained, by and upon the Oaths of a Jury of Twelve indifferent Men of one, ſome, or all of the Pariſhes in

which

which the said Roads lie (which Oath the said Trustees, or any Three or more of them, are hereby impowered to administer), what Damages such Owners, Occupiers, or Proprietors, or other Person or Persons interested or concerned therein, shall or may suffer or sustain for or by reason of the taking of any such Land, Ground, Tenements, or Hereditaments, into the said Roads, and what Recompence or Satisfaction such Owners, Occupiers, Proprietors, or other Person or Persons suffering thereby, shall respectively have by reason or on account thereof And for that Purpose, and in order thereto, the said Trustees, or any Seven or more of them, are hereby impowered and required, from time to time, as Occasion shall be or require, to summon and call before them all and every Person and Persons whatsoever, who shall be thought necessary or proper to be examined as Witness or Witnesses touching or concerning the Premises, and shall examine all such Witnesses before the said Jury, upon Oath (which Oath the said Trustees, or any Three or more of them, are hereby impowered and required to administer) And they shall also order and cause the said Jury to view the said Places in question, and to use all other lawful Ways and Means, as well for their own, as the said Jury's Information in the Premises, as they the said Trustees, or any Seven or more of them, shall think fit And after the said Jury shall have so inquired of, ascertained, and settled, such Damages and Recompence, they the said Trustees, or any Seven or more

of

of them, shall thereupon order, adjudge, and determine, the Sum or Sums of Money so assessed, by the said Jury, to be paid to the said Owners, Occupiers, or Proprietors, of the said Land, Ground, Tenements, and Hereditaments, or other Persons interested therein, according to such the Verdict or Inquisition of the said Jury, which said Verdict or Inquisition, and Judgment, Order, or Determination, so had and made, shall be final, and binding and conclusive, to all Intents and Purposes, against all Parties or Persons whatsoever claiming in Possession, Reversion, Remainder, or otherwise, their Heirs and Successors, as well absent as present, Infants, Feme Covert, and Persons under any other Disabilities whatsoever, Bodies Politick, Corporate, and Collegiate, as well as all other Person and Persons whomsoever, and all and every such Owners, Occupiers, and Proprietors, and all and every Person and Persons any-way interested in such Land, Grounds, Tenements, and Hereditaments, shall thereby be from thenceforth, to all Intents and Purposes, divested of all Right, Title, Claim, Interest, or Property, of, in, to, or out of the same. And, for the summoning and returning such Jury or Juries, the said Trustees, or any Seven or more of them, are hereby impowered to issue out their Warrant or Warrants to the Sheriff of the said County of *Wilts*, thereby commanding or requiring him to impanel, summon, and return, an indifferent Jury of Twenty-four Persons, to appear before the said Trustees, or any Seven

or

or more of them, at such time and Place as
in such Warrant shall be appointed, are
hereby required thereupon to summon, summon, and return, such Twenty-four Persons
accordingly, and, out of the Persons so
impannelled, summoned, and returned, or out of
such of them as shall appear according to or
upon such Summons, the said Trustees, or
any Three or more of them, shall cause, or
cause to be sworn, Twelve, who shall be the
Jury for the Purposes aforesaid. And, in Default of a sufficient Number of Jurymen, the
said Sheriff, or his Deputy, or Deputies, shall
return other honest and indifferent Men of
the standers-by, or that can be speedily
procured, to do such other service, to the Number of Twelve.

_Provided always, and be it further E-
nacted, by the Authority aforesaid, That
all Persons concerned shall, from time to time,
have their lawful Challenges against any of
the said Jurymen, when they come to be
sworn. And that the said Trustees, or any
Seven or more of them, acting in the Premises, shall have Power, from time to time,
to impose any reasonable Fine or Fines on
such Sheriff, his Deputy or Deputies, Bailiffs
or Agents, making Default in the Premises,
and on any of the Persons that shall be summoned and returned on such Jury, not appear-
ing, or refusing to be sworn on the said Jury,
and, being so sworn, and refusing, and no
giving their Verdict concerning the same, or
in any other manner wilfully neglecting their

C   Duties

Duties therein, contrary to the true Intent and Meaning of this Act; and on any Person or Persons, who, being required to give Evidence before the said Jury, touching the Premises, shall refuse to be examined, or to give Evidence, touching the same, and from time to time to impose such Fine or Fines, in such manner as any Fine is, by this present Act, directed to be levied and taken, no such Sum to exceed the Sum of Five Pounds upon any One Person, and all such Fines shall be employed for such Uses, and in such Manner, as the said Tolls or Moneys granted by this Act are to be laid out and applied.

And be it further Enacted, by the Authority aforesaid, That all and every such Sum and Sums of Money, Consideration, Recompence, or Satisfaction, to be agreed for, ascertained, or assessed, as aforesaid, shall be, and are hereby, charged and chargeable upon all Tolls which shall be raised and received on the said Roads; and the Moneys borrowed on the Credit thereof shall be paid thereout accordingly, to the Persons respectively intitled thereto, or to their respective Agents. And that, upon Payment or Tender thereof to the said Persons so respectively intitled thereto; and, in case of Refusal to accept the same, then upon leaving the same in the Hands of the Clerk, for the Time being, of the Trustees, for the Use of such Person or Persons as the said Trustees, or any Five or more of them, shall appoint the same to be paid unto, and after Three Months Notice

thereof

thereof given to such Person or Persons, it shall and may be lawful for the said Trustees, or any Five or more of them, their Surveyors, Workmen, and Agents, to take into, and add to, the said Roads, such Ground, Lands, or Tenements and to do all and every such Act, Matter, and Thing, with relation to the said Ground, Land, Tenements, and Hereditaments, so taken into and added, or to be taken into and added, to the said Roads, and to ditch and fence out the same, as the said Trustees, or any Five or more of them, shall think fit. And the said Ground or Grounds, Lands, or Tenements, so taken or to be taken in, when the same shall be so ditched and fenced, as aforesaid, shall, to all Intents and Purposes whatsoever, from thenceforth become and be, and shall be deemed and taken to be, a publick and common Highway, and be from thenceforth Part of the said Roads, not only during the Continuance of this present Act, but for ever after, and shall be repaired, and kept in Repair, by such Ways and Methods, and in all respects in such manner, as other Highways are, by Law, to be repaired, and kept in Repair.

and ditch and drain the same, and make a common Highway thereof.

And it is hereby Enacted and Declared, That, immediately after such Purchase and Conveyance made, the same Lands and Grounds, so to be purchased, shall be for ever deemed, used, and applied, as and for Part of such Highways or Roads accordingly.

The Lands, so purchased, to be deemed as Part of the said Roads.

Provided always, That in case the antient or former Way over any Moor or Waste-ground, or other Place, shall, by virtue or in pursuance of this Act, be turned or diverted, the Inhabitants of the Township, Parish, or Hamlet, wherein the old Road, which shall thereby be left or discontinued, shall lie, shall not be obliged to repair such old Road, unless the said old Road lead to some other Village, Town, or Place, than the new Road doth.

And, for preventing Frauds and Abuses in the said Tolls and Duties hereby granted, **Be it further Enacted,** by the Authority aforesaid, That if any Person or Persons, having paid the Toll or Duty by this Act laid, and having a Note or Ticket, Notes or Tickets, signifying the Payment of such Toll or Duty, shall give or dispose of the same Note or Notes, Ticket or Tickets, to any other Person or Persons, in order to avoid the Payment of the said Toll or Duty, every such Person giving or disposing of such Note or Ticket, Notes or Tickets, and the Person receiving the same, being thereof convicted, upon Oath, before the said Trustees, or any Five or more of them, or before One or more Justices of the Peace for the said County of *Wilts*, which Oath the said Trustees, or any Five or more of them, or the said Justice or Justices, is and are hereby impowered and required to administer, shall respectively forfeit and pay the Sum of

Twenty

Twenty Shillings, to be levied, recovered,
and disposed of, as any other Penalty or For-
forfeiture is hereby directed to be levied, recovered, and disposed of.

**P2ovided always, and it is hereby
Declared,** That no Person or Persons shall
be charged with any of the Tolls or Duties
aforesaid, for passing through any of the
Turnpikes to be erected by this Act, and
carrying any Quantities of Stones, Brick,
Lime, Timber, Wood, Gravel, or other
Materials for repairing the said Roads, or for
carrying through any of the said Turnpikes,
any Dung, Mould, or Compost, of any Nature or Kind whatsoever, for Manuring of
Lands or Gardens, nor shall any Toll or
Duty be demanded or taken, by virtue of
this Act, for any Carts, Wains, Waggons,
or other Carriages, carrying any Hay, or
Corn in the Straw, to be laid up in the
Houses, Outhouses, Barns, or Yards, of or
belonging to the respective Inhabitants of the
several Parishes, Townships, or Places, in
which the said Roads, hereby intended to be
repaired, do lie; nor for any Ploughs, Har-
rows, or any other Implements of Husbandry,
or any other thing whatsoever belonging to,
or employed by such Inhabitants respectively, in Husbandry, Manuring or Stocking of
Lands lying near the said Roads; nor shall
any of the Tolls or Duties hereby laid be demanded or taken from any Person or Persons
residing in the said Parishes in which the said
Roads, hereby directed to be repaired, do lie,

*Persons and
Things exempt
from Tolls*

C 3 who

who fhall pafs through the faid Turnpikes to
and from Church, Chapel, or other Places of
religious Worfhip, on *Sundays*, or who fhall
attend the Funeral of any Perfon or Perfons
who fhall die, or be buried, in any of the
Parifhes in which the faid Roads, hereby directed to be repaired, do lie, or for any
Horfes, Geldings, Mares, or Cattle, going
to, or returning from, Pafture or Watering-
places, belonging to fuch Parifhes, Townfhips,
or Places, or any of the neighbouring Inhabitants near the faid Roads, or for any Poft-
horfes carrying the Mail or Packet; nor fhall
any Toll or Duty be demanded or taken for
the Horfes of Soldiers paffing, who are upon
their March, or for Carts, Carriages, or
Waggons, attending them, or laden with
their Arms or Baggage; or for Horfes,
Carts, or Waggons, travelling with Vagrants
fent by legal Paffes.

𝕬𝖓𝖉 𝖇𝖊 𝖎𝖙 𝖋𝖚𝖗𝖙𝖍𝖊𝖗 𝕰𝖓𝖆𝖈𝖙𝖊𝖉, by the Authority aforefaid, That the Right and Property of all and every the Turnpikes and
Toll-houfes, which fhall be erected and built
by virtue of this Act, fhall be vefted in the
faid Truftees appointed, or to be appointed,
to put the fame in Execution, and that they,
or any Seven or more of them, are hereby
authorized and impowered to difpofe thereof
as they fhall think proper; or to bring Actions, or prefer Bills of Indictment, in their
Names, or in the Name or Names of their
Clerk or Clerks, Treafurer or Treafurers, or
any One or more of them, againft any Perfon

or

or Perſons who ſhall ſteal, take away, break down, or ſpoil, ſuch Turnpikes or Toll-houſes, or any or either of them, ſo directed to be built, as aforeſaid.

Provided always, and be it further Enacted, by the Authority aforeſaid, That all and every Perſon and Perſons, who, by Law, are chargeable towards the repairing and amending the ſaid Roads hereby intended to be repaired, ſhall ſtill remain chargeable, and do their reſpective Days Works in the ſaid Pariſhes, Townſhips, or Places, in which the ſaid Roads do lie, in ſuch manner as he, ſhe, or they, ought to have done before the Paſſing of this Act.

Perſons chargeable to the Highway, to continue ſo.

And, for preventing Differences which may ariſe between the ſaid Truſtees and the Surveyors of the Highways, for the Time being, for the ſeveral Pariſhes and Places through which the Roads aforeſaid do lead, touching what Part of the Statute-work in any Pariſh, Place, or Diviſion, ought to be done on the Roads by this Act directed to be repaired; Be it further Enacted, by the Authority aforeſaid, That it ſhall and may be lawful for the Juſtices of the Peace, at any of their General or Petty Seſſions, to be held for any of the Diviſions in which the ſaid Roads do lie, upon Application made to them by the ſaid Truſtees, or any Five or more of them, to adjudge and determine what Part or Proportion of the Statute-work ſhall be done, in the Roads aforeſaid, by the

Power for Juſtices to direct the Proportions of Statute Works, on Application

C 4   Inha-

Inhabitants of each or any of the Parishes or Tythings in which the said Roads, hereby directed to be amended, do lie.

Provided also, and be it further Enacted, by the Authority aforesaid, That it shall and may be lawful to and for the said Trustees, or any Five or more of them, from time to time, during the Continuance of this Act, to compound and agree with any of the Parishes, Tythings, or Townships, to which the said Roads do belong, or with any of the Owners, Possessors, or Occupiers, of such Lands, Tenements, or Hereditaments, as are or shall be liable or chargeable to the Repair of any Part of the said Roads, for a certain Sum of Money, or Land, or Ground, adjoining to the said Roads, to be laid into the same, or otherwise by the Year, as the said Trustees, or any Five or more of them, shall think reasonable, in lieu of the Statute or other Work, or Repairs, to be done by such Parish or Parishes, Township or Townships, Tything or Tythings, or by such Owner or Owners, Possessor or Possessors, Occupier or Occupiers, of such Lands, Tenements, and Hereditaments, chargeable as aforesaid; Copies of all which Compositions or Agreements, so to be made by the said Trustees, as aforesaid, shall be entered at Length in a Book or Books, to be kept for that Purpose by the said Clerk or Clerks, Treasurer or Treasurers, which said Book or Books shall and may, at all seasonable times, be seen and perused by

any

any Perſon or Perſons whomſoever, without Fee or Reward.

And be it further Enacted, by the Authority aforeſaid, That the reſpective Surveyor or Surveyor of the ſaid Roads, for the Time being, of all and every the Pariſh and Pariſhes, in which the ſaid Roads, intended to be repaired by this preſent Act, do lie, ſhall yearly and every Year, during the Continuance of this Act, within Ten Days after Demand made to him or them, in Writing, by the Turnpike-Surveyor or Surveyors appointed or to be appointed by the ſaid Truſtees, or any Five or more of them, give and deliver to the ſaid Turnpike-Surveyor or Surveyors, an exact Liſt or Account in Writing under his or their Hands, of the Chriſtian and Surnames of all and every Perſon and Perſons in the ſaid reſpective Pariſhes and Places, who are, by Law, chargeable towards repairing the Roads in any of the ſaid Pariſhes; and ſhall ſet forth and ſpecify in ſuch Liſt what each Perſon is reſpectively chargeable with, for and towards the ſame; and the ſaid Pariſh-Surveyor or Surveyors, for the Time being, reſpectively, within Ten Days after Notice ſhall be given them, or either of them, by the ſaid Turnpike-Surveyor or Surveyors, of the time when, and how many of the Perſons, ſo chargeable as aforeſaid, he or they would have to do ſuch their reſpective Statute or Days Work, ſo adjudged or appointed as aforeſaid, in and upon any Part or Parts of the ſaid Roads,

ſhall

shall summon or give publick Notice thereof to the said Person or Persons, so chargeable as aforesaid: And if any Parish-Surveyor or Surveyors aforesaid shall neglect or refuse to do as they are hereby required and directed to do, he or they, for every such Neglect or Refusal, shall forfeit and pay the Sum of Ten Pounds: And if any Person or Persons keeping a Team or Teams, Draught or Draughts, Cart or Carts, and chargeable towards repairing the said Roads, shall, after such Summons, or publick Notice, neglect or refuse to send their respective Teams, Draughts, or Carts, to do and perform such their respective Days Work on the said Roads, he, she, or they, so neglecting or refusing, shall respectively forfeit and pay the Sum of Ten Shillings for every Team, Draught, or Cart, making Default each of the said respective Days: And if any Labourer, or other Person or Persons so chargeable towards repairing the said Roads, shall, at any time, neglect or refuse (after such Summons, or publick Notice) to do and perform the said appointed Days Work on the said Roads, he, she, or they, shall respectively forfeit and pay the Sum of One Shilling and Six-pence for each of the said Days such Labourer, or other Person or Persons, shall make Default: And if any Person or Persons, who shall (according to such Summons, or publick Notice, as aforesaid) come to Work, as Labourers, or be sent with any Team, Draught, or Cart, to work on the said Roads, are found idle or negligent by the said Turnpike-Surveyor or Surveyors respectively,

Penalty on Neglect

Penalty on Persons not doing their statute-work

Persons coming to Work, and being negligent, to be turned off,

spectively, where the Work is to be done;
in such Case, the said Turnpike-Surveyor or
Surveyors may, and is and are hereby impowered and required to remove and turn
him or them off, who shall be found idle or
negligent, as aforesaid, and it shall be esteemed as if such Person or Persons had not come,
or sent any Team, Draught, or Cart, to
work on the said Roads; and he, she, or
they, shall be subject and liable to the respective Forfeitures and Payments afore-men-
tioned, as if he, she, or they, had neglected
or refused to do or perform the said respective Days Work, so ordered and appointed,
as aforesaid.

*And liable to
Punishment for
such Neglect.*

**Provided always, and be it further
Enacted,** by the Authority aforesaid, That
if any of the Surveyors of the Highways of
and for such Parish, Township, or Hamlet, for which any such Composition shall be
made for any Statute or Days Work, as aforesaid, shall pay the Composition-money, or in
case such Composition-money shall be levied
on him, in the manner herein before provided, all and every such Surveyor and Surveyors shall and may be reimbursed the Composition-money he shall so pay, or which
shall be so levied on him, together with the
Charges of the same, in such manner as, by
the Laws now in being, Surveyors of the
Highways of this Kingdom are to be reimbursed the Moneys by them expended, in
buying Materials for amending the said Highways.

*Surveyors paying
in Composition-
money, how to be
reimbursed.*

Pro-

Provided always, and it is further Enacted, That if it shall appear to the said Trustees, or any Seven or more of them, that any Lands, Tenements, or Hereditaments, or the Rents and Profits arising out of any Lands, Tenements, or Hereditaments, now are, or hereafter shall be, liable and chargeable towards the amending the Road by this Act directed to be amended, such Lands, Tenements, and Hereditaments, shall still remain liable and chargeable, and the Possessors and Occupiers of such Lands, Tenements, and Hereditaments, are hereby required and directed to pay such Rents and Profits to such Person or Persons as the said Trustees, or any Seven or more of them, shall appoint to receive the several Duties granted by this Act; and upon Default of Payment thereof, it shall and may be lawful to and for the said Trustees, or any Seven or more of them, by Warrant under their Hands and Seals, to levy the same by Distress and Sale of the Goods of such Person or Persons as shall neglect or refuse to make such Payment, as aforesaid; and such Rents and Profits, when recovered and received, shall be applied, from time to time, for and towards amending the said Road, and to no other Use or Purpose whatsoever.

Provided always, and it is further Enacted, That the setting down of Stone for any Purpose, and erecting, the setting up of any Posts, &c.

Bodies Politick and Corporate, to any such Person or Persons there, by long Usage, been had, and lawfully taken, upon any Part of the said Road.

And be it further Enacted, by the Authority aforesaid, That all Penalties and Forfeitures, by this Act incurred (touching which no other Provision is herein made, shall be recovered and levied by Distress and Sale of the Offender's Goods and Chattels, by Warrant or Warrants under the Hands and Seals of One or more of his Majesty's Justices of the Peace for the said County or Town (which Warrant or Warrants, the said Justices are hereby impowered and required to issue, upon Information of One or more credible Witness or Witnesses, upon Oath, which Oath the said Justices are hereby impowered and required to administer without Fee or Reward; and the Penalties and Forfeitures when recovered, after rendering the Overplus, if any be, to the Party or Parties whose Goods and Chattels shall be so distrained and sold, the Charges of the said Distress and Sale being first deducted, shall go, and be applied and laid out, if not otherwise applied and disposed of by this Act, for and towards amending the said Road.

And be it further enacted, and it is hereby Enacted, by the Authority aforesaid, That all Orders and proceedings of the Trustees shall be entered into a Book or Books to be kept for that purpose, and such Orders to which shall be signed by the Clerk to the said Trustees, at any Meeting of Trustees, or of the Trustees aforesaid assembled, as the Case shall require. And such Orders shall be esteemed and taken to be good and valid, as if the same were under the Hands and Seals of the said majority of the said Trustees. Which said Orders or Books, and also the said Book directed to be kept in the Library by the said Affidavits or otherwise, shall and may be produced, or used in Evidence, in all Cases of Appeals, or on Actions touching any thing done or transacted, in or by the Authority, of this Act.

And it is hereby further Enacted by the Authority aforesaid, That in case any Collector or Collectors, Receiver or Receivers, Person or Persons, or any or either of them, or Party or Parties, finding him, her, or themselves, aggrieved by any thing done in pursuance of this Act, it shall and may be lawful to and for him, her, or them, within the Space of Six Months, to appeal to the Justices of the Peace, at their next General Quarter Sessions of the Peace to be held in the said County of ———, who are hereby authorised and required to take Cognizance thereof, and to hear and determine the Complaint or Complaints of any Person or Persons, so aggrieved, and, if they see Cause, shall and may, by Order of such Sessions, mitigate, at their Discretion, all or any the Penalties had or incurred by the Party or Parties complaining, or may confirm or set aside the said Conviction or Convictions, Commitment or

... Commissioners, and for the Parties to ... lany, or otherwise ... first had and obtain such Conversion or Conversions as shall be made, by the Person or Persons so appealing, as aforesaid, they ... are hereby directed to give Notice, in Writing, to the Treasurer or Treasurers, for the Time being, of the Tolls and Duties granted by this Act, of the said intended ... be ... or prosecuting ... and ... within Three ... or ... Notice given, enter into a ... by some Justice of the Peace for the said County or ... with two ... to try such Appeal ... the ... ... of the ... ... shall ... ... Councils or ... ... and ... ... and ... upon such Appeal ... and such Appeal and ... ... at the ... next General Quarter Session, be there heard, and finally determined.

And be it ... enacted, and be it further enacted, by the Authority aforesaid, That no Order made touching or concerning any of the Matters aforesaid, or any other Proceedings to be had touching the Conviction or Convictions of any Offender or Offenders against this present Act, shall be quashed or vacated for want of Form only, or be removed or removable by Certiorari, or any other Writ or Process whatsoever, into any of his Majesty's Courts of Record at ...; any thing herein contained to the contrary notwithstanding.

And be it further Enacted by the Authority aforesaid, That the Tolls and Duties hereby granted shall take Place on and after the First Day of May, One thousand Seven hundred and Fifty two, and shall continue and be paid, from thenceforth, for and during the Term of Twenty-one Years, and from thence to the End of the then next Session of Parliament. But if at any Time before the Expiration of the said Term, all the said Roads shall be sufficiently mended and repaired, and so adjudged by the Justices of the Peace for the said County of Herts, at their General Quarterly Sessions, to be next after Easter, that then, from and after such Adjudication made, and Repayment of all such Monies as shall have been borrowed on the Credit of the said Tolls and Duties hereby granted, with the Interest for the same, and the Costs and Charges thereof, and of obtaining this Act of Parliament the aforesaid Tolls and Duties (other than and except such Tolls and Duties as are hereby established and confirmed to, and vested in, *George Dale* and *Moses Castle* herein after-named, or the Owner or Owners of *Stoke* Bridge, erected at *Stoke-*ton, for the time being), shall cease and determine, any thing herein contained to the contrary notwithstanding.

And be it further Enacted and Decreed, by the Authority aforesaid, That it shall be any Lawful to and for any of the said Trustees appointed or to be appointed to

put

put this Act in Execution, who is, are, or shall be, in the Commission of the Peace for the said County of *Wilts*, to act as a Justice or Justices of the Peace, in all Cases, Matters, and Things, as may be necessary for the more speedy and effectual putting in Execution the several Authorities and Powers in this Act mentioned and contained.

And, for continuing a sufficient Number of Trustees to put this Act in Execution, **Be it further Enacted,** by the Authority aforesaid, That when and as often as any Trustee or Trustees shall die, remove, or refuse to act, it shall and may be lawful for such of the said Trustees, as shall survive and remain, or any Seven or more of them, by any Writing or Writings under their Hands and Seals, from time to time, during the Continuance of the Term hereby granted, to elect, nominate, and appoint, One or more fit Person or Persons, living in the said County of *Wilts*, in the room and place of such Trustee or Trustees so dying, removed, or refusing to act, and such Person or Persons so elected, nominated, and appointed, shall be joined with such surviving or remaining Trustees in Execution of all and every the Powers in them reposed, by virtue of this Act. And Notice of the Time and Place of Meeting, for the Election of such new Trustee or Trustees, shall be given by the Clerk or Clerks to the said Trustees for the Time being, who is hereby required to fix, or cause to be fixed, such Notice, in Writing, at or on all the Turnpike-

D gates

gts which shall be erected, by virtue of this Act, at least Ten Days before the Meeting for such Election, and all and every such Person or Persons, as shall be chosen and appointed to be joined with such surviving or remaining Trustees, shall and may, and they are hereby authorized and impowered to act, to all Intents and Purposes, in as full, large, and ample Manner, as the said Trustees, nominated by this Act, are hereby authorized and impowered to act, and to do

And be it further Enacted, by the Authority aforesaid, That the said Trustees, or any Seven or more of them, shall meet at the House of *Mary Harding*, Widow, at the Sign of the *Old Bear*, in the Town of *Bradford*, on the Twentieth Day of *April* One thousand Seven hundred and Fifty-two, and then choose a Clerk or Clerks to write their Orders, and take Minutes, and make Entries of their Proceedings, and for other Purposes, and shall then adjourn themselves, and shall afterwards meet at the Place aforesaid, or at any other Place or Places in or near the said Roads so to be repaired, as the said Trustees, or any Five or more of them, shall think proper or convenient, as often as it shall be necessary for putting this Act in Execution. And if it shall happen, that there shall not appear at any Meeting, which shall be appointed to be held by the said Trustees, a sufficient Number of Trustees to act at such Meeting, and to adjourn to any other Day, then, and in such Case, the Clerk to the said Trustees, by Notice, in Writing under his Hand, to be fixed on all the said Turnpike-gates to be erected by virtue of this Act, at least Ten Days before the Meeting, shall appoint the said Trustees to meet at the House where the Meeting of the said Trustees was appointed to be held, or at some other convenient House near the said Roads, on that Day Three Weeks on which such last Meeting of the Trustees was appointed to be held, and that the said Trustees, at their first and all their subsequent Meetings, shall defray their own Charges and Expences.

Provided always, and be it further Declared and Enacted, That no Person or Persons appointed or to be appointed, by this Act, a Trustee or Trustees for putting this Act in Execution, shall have or accept of any Place of Profit arising out of it, or by reason of the Tolls or Duties by this Act laid or granted, but such Person or Persons shall be incapable of acting as a Trustee or Trustees, from the Time of Accepting, and during the Enjoyment, of such Place of Profit, as aforesaid.

Provided also, and it is hereby further Enacted, That the said Trustees, or any Five or more of them, shall and may, and they are hereby required to cause the said Roads to be measured, and Stones or Posts to be thereon, and in or near the Sides of the said Roads, erected, each Stone or Post at the Distance of One Mile from another, and denoting the Distances of every such Stone or

Post

Post from any other Place, as to the said Trustees, shall seem meet. And if any Person or Persons shall voluntarily and maliciously break any of the Stones or Posts, or any Part thereof, which shall be so erected and set up, or shall obliterate or deface any of the Words, Letters, Figures, or Marks, which shall be engraved or inscribed thereon, and shall be convicted thereof by the Confession of the Party, or by the Oath of One or more credible Witness or Witnesses, before One or more Justices of the Peace for the said County of Wilts, every such Person or Persons so offending shall forfeit and pay the Sum of Forty Shillings, to be levied by Distress and Sale of the Goods and Chattels of every such Offender, by Warrant under the Hand and Seal, or Hands and Seals, of the Justice or Justices before whom such Conviction shall be made, such Forfeitures to be applied in repairing the Stones and Posts so broken and defaced, or in supplying new ones in their stead. And if there shall be any Overplus of such Forfeitures, the same shall be laid out in the Repair of the said Road. And in case the Person or Persons so offending, and convicted, shall have no Goods and Chattels, then it shall and may be lawful to and for any One or more of such Justice or Justices, by Warrant under his Hand and Seal, or their Hands and Seals, to commit such Person or Persons to the Common Gaol of the said County of Wilts, for the Space of One Month, and the Person or Persons so offending, and convicted, shall not be discharged

until

until he, she, or they, shall have paid the
Sum of Forty Shillings, or until the Expiration of the said One Month.

Provided always, and it is hereby
Declared. That no Money shall be borrowed, by the said Trustees, on the Credit of the
Tolls to be collected after such Meeting, unless Notice be, for that Purpose, fixed, in
Writing under the Hand of the Clerk to the
said Trustees, upon all the Turnpike-gates to be
erected by virtue of this Act, at least Twenty
Days before the borrowing such Money.

Provided also, and be it further Enacted, by the Authority aforesaid, That no
Nomination, Appointment, Information, Order, Judgment, Conviction, Warrant, or other
Writing whatsoever, under the Hand and
Seal, or Hands and Seals, of, or only signed
by, any Trustee or Trustees for putting this
Act in Execution, or any Justice or Justices
of the Peace, or exhibited before them, or
any of them, touching, concerning, or in Execution of, any Power or Authority hereby
vested in such Trustees, or Justices of the
Peace, or any of them, shall be charged or
chargeable with any Stamp-Duty whatsoever

And it is also further Enacted. by the
Authority aforesaid, That all and every Per-
son or Persons, to whom any Assignment or
Assignments shall be made, by the said Trus-

D 3 tees,

tees, or any Seven or more of them, as a
Security for any Sum or Sums of Money,
by any Perfon or Perfons lent and advanced
on the Credit, and for the Purpofes mentioned in this Act, or who fhall be intitled to
the Money thereby fecured, fhall and may,
from time to time, by proper Words of Affignment, to be indorfed on the Back of his, her,
or their Security, or by any other Writing or
Writings, under his, her, or their Hands and
Seals, to be duly executed in the Prefence
of Two or more credible Witneffes, affign or
transfer his, her, or their Right, Title, In-
tereft, or Benefit, to the Principal and In-
tereft-money thereby fecured, or any Part
thereof, to any Perfon or Perfons whomfo-
ever, which faid Transfer or Affignment
fhall be produced and notified to the faid
Clerk or Clerks, Treafurer or Treafurers, appointed or to be appointed by the faid Truftees, or any Seven or more of them, within
Three Months after the Date thereof, who
fhall caufe an Entry or Memorial to be made
of fuch Affignment or Transfer, containing
the Date, Parties, and Sum of Money therein
mentioned to be transferred, in the faid Book
to be kept for the entering the faid original
Affignments, for which the faid Clerk or
Clerks, Treafurer or Treafurers, fhall be
paid the Sum of Two Shillings, and no more.
And, after fuch Entry made, fuch Affignment
fhall intitle fuch Affignee, his, her, and their
Executors, Adminiftrators, and Affigns, to
the

the Benefit thereof, and Payment thereon, and such Assignee may, in like manner, assign again, and so *toties quoties*, and it shall not be in the Power of such Person or Persons, who shall have made such Assignment, to make void, release, or discharge the same, or any Moneys thereby due, or any Part thereof.

Provided always, and be it further Enacted, by the Authority aforesaid, That if any Action or Suit shall be commenced against any Person or Persons, for any thing to be done in pursuance of this Act, every such Action or Suit shall be brought within Four Months next after the Fact committed, and not afterwards, and shall be laid in the said County of *Wilts*, and not elsewhere. And the Defendant or Defendants, in such Action or Suit, shall and may plead the General Issue, Not Guilty, and give this Act, and the special Matter, in Evidence, at any Tryal to be had thereupon, and that the same was done in Pursuance, and by the Authority, of this Act. And if it shall appear so to be done, or that such Action or Suit shall be brought in any other County, Place, or Places, that then the Jury shall find for the Defendant or Defendants. And upon such Verdict, or if the Plaintiff or Plaintiffs shall become Nonsuited, or discontinue his Action, after the Defendant or Defendants shall have appeared, or if, upon Demurrer, Judgment shall be given

against

against the Plaintiff or Plaintiff, the Defendant or Defendants shall and may recover
treble Costs, , and have such Remedy for
the same, as any Defendant or Defendants
have or have in any Case by Law

And it is further Enacted, by the Authority aforesaid, That this Act shall be
deemed, adjudged, and taken, to be a Publick
Act, and be judicially taken Notice of as
such by all Judges, Justices, and other Persons whatsoever, without specially pleading
the same

And Whereas by Articles of Agreement,
bearing Date the Twelfth Day of July One
thousand seven hundred and Thirty-one, and
made between John Teacher, Thomas Methuen,
. . Cooper, and John Long, Liquires, and others
Inhabitants of, and Owners and Proprietors
of Lands and Tenements in the Tything of
. . . aforesaid, of the one Part, and Thomas Dyke, of Landry boke, in the Parish of
F . . . in the County of Wilts, Gentleman, and Moses Castle the elder, of Winsley
in the same County, Gentleman, of the other
Part, after reciting therein, That a Bridge
was intended to be erected over the River
Avon, at or near a Place called Stokeford, in
the County of Wilts, by the said Thomas
Dyke and Moses Castle, or one of them, at
his or their own proper Costs and Charges;
and that for some time past a Way had been
used for Horse and Foot-passengers, leading
from

from *Bradford* to the City of *Bath*, through
the said River *Avon*, at *Stokeford* aforesaid;
but that some Doubts had arisen, whether
there was or had been any good Right or
Title for such Passengers to go, pass, or repass, in, by, and through the said Way;
To the End, therefore, that all Doubts and
Scruples might, for ever after the Erecting
of such Bridge, be removed, touching or
concerning the said Way, it was agreed, by
and between all the Parties to the said Articles, That the Way leading from *Bradford*
to *Stokeford* aforesaid should, immediately
after the said Bridge should be built, be at
all times deemed and taken as and for a publick and common Highway and Road, to all
Intents and Purposes, for all Coaches, Waggons, Wains, Carts, Carriages, Horses, Oxen,
Cows, Sheep, Pigs, and all other Cattle whatsoever, and that the same Way and Road
should, at all times, and for ever after the
erecting such Bridge, be repaired and re-
pairable by the publick Statute-labour, and
at the common Costs and Charges of the Inhabitants and Land-owners within the Tything of *Winfley* aforesaid, and not at the Costs
and Charges of any particular Owner or Owners, Tenant or Tenants, of Land then inclosed, or thereafter to be inclosed, lying adjacent to the said Road, and the said Inhabitants and Land-owners of and in *Winfley*
aforesaid, Parties to the said Articles, did
thereby agree to pay a Toll for the Passage
over

over the said Bridge, not to exceed One Shilling for a Coach, Chariot, or Waggon, and
Six-pence for every Cart or Wain, and One
Peny for each Horse, and an Halfpeny for
each Passenger, and Five pence for each
Score of Sheep, Lambs, and Pigs, and an
Halfpeny for each Bull, Ox, or Cow, and
so in proportion, for every greater Number
of Cattle.

And whereas the said *Thomas Dike*, and
Moses Cottle the elder, did afterwards, at their
own Expence, whereof Three-fourth Parts
was paid by the said *Thomas Dike*, and One-
fourth Part by the said *Moses Cottle*, erect
and build such Bridge, near *Stokeford* aforesaid, and a little House or Tenement near
the said Bridge, for the Habitation of a Person to collect the Tolls for the Passage over
the same, and they, and their Representa-
tives, have ever since, at their own Expence,
maintained and kept, as well the same Bridge,
as also such Part of the Road intended to be
repaired by this Act, as lies between *Comb-
bridge* aforesaid and *Rowass-gate*, in the Tything of *Winsley* aforesaid, in good Order and
Repair, and have taken and received at the
same Bridge, for their own Use, the several
Tolls and Duties herein after-mentioned,
that is to say, For every Waggon, Coach,
Chariot, or other Four-wheel Carriage, One
Shilling, For every Cart, Chaise, or other
Two-wheel Carriage, Six-pence, For any
Horse, Mule, or Ass, One Peny, For every
Ox, Cow, or other Neat Cattle, an Half-
peny,

pens, For every Score of Sheep, Lambs, or Pigs, Five-pence; and for every Foot-passenger, an Halfpeny: And *George Dike*, Gentleman, lawful Representative of the said *Thomas Dike*, and *Moses Cottle*, Son and Heir of the said *Moses Cottle* the Father, are willing and desirous to undertake and continue to repair and support the said Bridge, and such Part of the said Road, as aforesaid, so as the Tolls and Duties so taken at the said Bridge, as aforesaid, be established and continued to such Person or Persons as now are, or shall, for the Time being, be Owner or Owners of the said Bridge so erected, as aforesaid, according to their several and respective Interests therein:

Now it is hereby further Enacted and Declared, That all that Part of the Road intended to be repaired by this Act, which lies between *Conve-bridge* and *Roways-gate* aforesaid, and through *Machell-mead*, shall, from time to time, and at all times hereafter for ever, be used, deemed, and taken, to all Intents and Purposes, to be a publick or common Highway, as well for all Carts and Carriages whatsoever, as for Horses, and other Cattle

And it is hereby further Enacted and Declared, That the said Tolls and Duties herein before-mentioned to have been taken by the said *Thomas Dike*, and *Moses Cottle* the elder, at *Dike-bridge* aforesaid, shall be, and the same are hereby, established and confirmed

firmed to, and are hereby vested in, and shall and may be taken and received by, the said *George Dike* and *Moses Cottle*, or the Owner or Owners of the said Bridge, for the Time being, they respectively supporting and maintaining the said Bridge, and keeping the same, and also the said Road, lying between *Combe-bridge* and *Rowass-gate* aforesaid, in good Order and Repair, at their respective own Costs and Charges, according to their respective Interests in the said Bridge

And it is hereby further Enacted and Declared, That the said *George Dike* and *Moses Cottle*, and the Owner or Owners of the said Bridge, for the Time being, shall and may have, use, and enjoy, such Powers and Remedies for levying, recovering, and receiveing, the said Tolls and Duties, and enforcing the Payment thereof, as the said Trustees have, or can or may have, use, exercise, or put in force, for the recovering any of the Tolls or Duties directed to be levied and paid by this Act.

Provided always, and it is hereby Enacted and Declared, That in case at any time, during the Continuance of this present Act, the said *George Dike* and *Moses Cottle*, or the Owner or Owners of the said Bridge, for the Time being, shall neglect or refuse to maintain and support the said Bridge, and keep the same, and such Part of the said Road, as aforesaid, in good Order and Repair, upon Three Months Notice, in Writing,

Writing, to be given to them the said *George Dike* and *Moses Cottle*, or the Owner or Owners of the said Bridge, for the Time being, respectively, by the said Trustees appointed, or to be appointed, by this Act, or their Successors, or any Seven or more of them, it shall and may be lawful to and for the said Trustees nominated and appointed by this Act, and their Successors, or any Seven or more of them, or such Person or Persons as they respectively shall in that behalf depute or appoint, to enter into and upon the said Toll-house or Tenement, and the Turnpike or Toll-gate erected and set up at *Stokebridge* aforesaid, and to receive, collect, and take, the Tolls and Duties directed and appointed by this Act to be there levied and paid, as aforesaid ; and to apply and dispose of the same, for the supporting and maintaining the said Bridge, and keeping the same, and such Part of the Road, as aforesaid, in good Order and Repair, until thereby, or therewith, or otherwise, the same Bridge, and that Part of the said Road, shall be effectually repaired and amended, and put into good Order and Repair, and no longer.

CPSIA information can be obtained
at www.ICGtesting.com
Printed in the USA
BVOW09s1702020418

512247BV00018B/666/P

9 781171 225935